D1085416

PUBLIC LIBRARY

CREEPY CREATURES

ALIENS

Big Buddy Books

An Imprint of Abdo Publishing
abdopublishing.com

Sarah Tieck

abdopublishing.com

Published by Abdo Publishing, a division of ABDO, PO Box 398166, Minneapolis, Minnesota 55439.
Copyright © 2016 by Abdo Consulting Group, Inc. International copyrights reserved in all countries. No part
of this book may be reproduced in any form without written permission from the publisher. Big Buddy Books™
is a trademark and logo of Abdo Publishing.

Printed in the United States of America, North Mankato, Minnesota.
042015
092015

THIS BOOK CONTAINS
RECYCLED MATERIALS

Cover Photo: © iStockphoto.com.
Interior Photos: AP Photo/Stocktrek Images (p. 13); ASSOCIATED PRESS (pp. 20, 21, 25); Hulton Archive/Getty Images
(p. 23); © iStockphoto.com (pp. 5, 7, 9, 11, 13, 15); © Moviestore collection Ltd/Alamy (p. 19); MyLoupe/Getty
Images (p. 27); NASA/JPL-Caltech/MSSS (p. 27); Paramount Pictures/Getty Images (p. 25); © Pictorial Press
Ltd/Alamy (p. 22); Shutterstock.com (pp. 20, 29, 30); Superstock/Glow Images (p. 17).

Coordinating Series Editor: Rochelle Baltzer
Contributing Editors: Tamara L. Britton, Bridget O'Brien, Marcia Zappa
Graphic Design: Jenny Christensen

Library of Congress Cataloging-in-Publication Data

Tieck, Sarah, 1976- author.
  Aliens / Sarah Tieck.
    pages cm. -- (Creepy creatures)
  ISBN 978-1-62403-763-4
 1. Extraterrestrial beings--Juvenile literature. 2. Unidentified flying objects--Juvenile literature. I. Title.
 TL789.2.T54 2016
 001.942--dc23
                        2015002629

Contents

Creepy Aliens

People love to tell spooky stories, especially about creepy creatures such as aliens. They tell of large alien eyes and slimy flesh. They report seeing **UFOs** whoosh through the sky!

Aliens have appeared in books, stories, plays, television shows, and movies. But are they real, or the stuff of **legend**? Let's find out more about aliens, and you can decide for yourself!

Did you know?

Aliens are also called *extraterrestrials*. This means "beyond Earth."

Some aliens are scary!

5

Scary Stories

The stories people tell usually describe aliens as unusual creatures from other planets. Some aliens resemble humans or even giant insects. Others are covered in wildly colored hair or toxic slime!

Aliens often have special abilities. Some can fly or control people's thoughts. Others speak an alien language. Or, they **communicate** using their minds.

Aliens have many different looks! This may include green skin and pointy ears.

The aliens in stories are from different planets. They travel in spaceships. They may be seeking food or other **resources** for their own dying planets. Some just want to kill humans or other **species**. Others plan to take over as many worlds as they can.

Stories describe alien intelligence and abilities. Often they have **technology** or skills far beyond what humans have. Aliens are hard to stop.

Did you know?

In many movies about alien attacks, people must destroy hundreds or thousands of aliens!

Alien spaceships may look quite different from Earth's space shuttles. And, they may be much larger!

Around the World

People from many **cultures** tell stories of aliens and **UFOs**. Certain historical structures are hard to explain. The stones used to build them were very heavy. And, some line up with compass points. This required advanced building methods. So, some people believe it was aliens who built them.

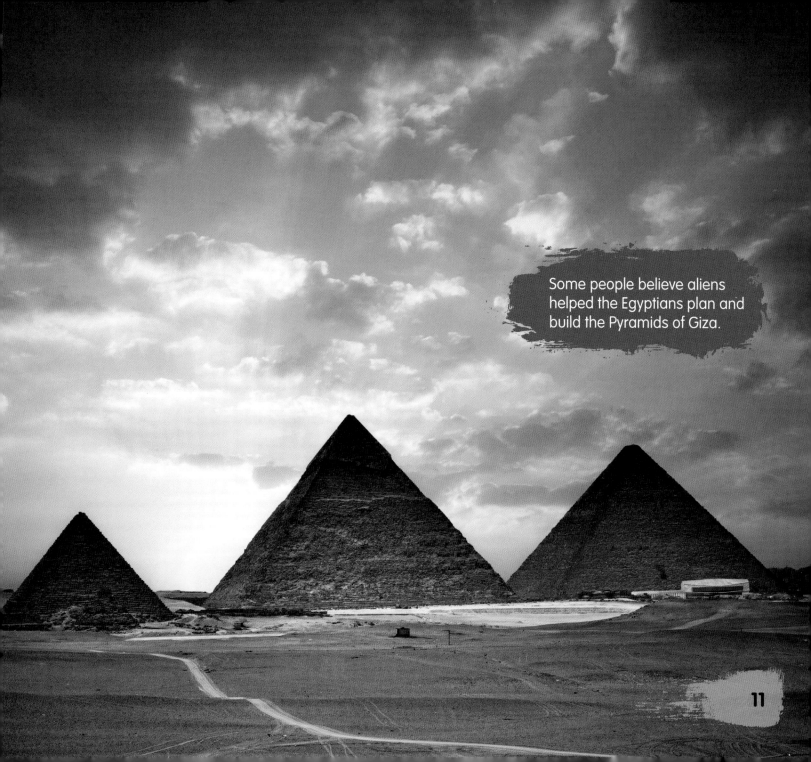

Some people believe aliens helped the Egyptians plan and build the Pyramids of Giza.

Some people believe aliens helped ancient **cultures** such as the Maya. Believing in aliens offers some explanation for the advanced ideas and buildings of the Maya.

Others believe aliens built stone circles in Europe. People have not been able to understand the purpose of these circles. And, some stones were from areas far away from where the circles were built.

Stonehenge is a famous stone circle in England. No one knows its purpose.

Some people believe aliens helped move the heavy stones used for Stonehenge.

Living History

Belief in aliens goes back thousands of years. For example, ancient writings from India describe flying machines. And, people have found drawings of possible aliens in caves and ancient buildings.

Large, unexplained designs have been found in farm fields, deserts, highlands, and islands around the world. These include crop circles and the Nazca Lines. These designs can best be seen from the air. So, some people believe aliens are responsible.

Large crop circles often appear overnight. People can't explain how they were made or by whom. So, some think aliens are responsible.

The Nazca Lines were created hundreds of years ago. Many form the shapes of huge animals.

With so many stories about **UFOs**, many people began looking for proof. In 1947, a farmer found strange objects on his land near Roswell, New Mexico. People believe they came from a UFO that had crash-landed near there.

Around the 1950s, different countries began to work to send ships into space. People became interested in the possibility of life on other planets. So aliens and spaceships began to appear in **science fiction**. Some of the stories were funny, while others were very scary.

Magazines of science fiction stories have been popular over the years.

Good or Evil?

No two groups of aliens are the same. Some are evil. They may steal **resources** from Earth. Others take people away in their spaceships. People must figure out how to fight against unusual alien abilities to save themselves and Earth.

Yet in other stories, aliens are good. They may be lost or hurt. Some are from a sick or dying planet. Others come to Earth to help save people or teach them new things.

Some aliens are kind. They may just want to learn more about humans and life on Earth.

Marvin the Martian

This *Looney Tunes* character appears in many cartoons. He wants to blow up Earth so he can see Venus better. His enemy is Bugs Bunny.

Spock

This famous alien first appeared in the 1960s television series *Star Trek*. Spock comes from the planet Vulcan. He helps make important decisions using reason instead of emotion. He is known for his pointy ears and the Vulcan salute (*above*).

Aliens in Pop Culture

Yoda

Yoda is one of many aliens in the Star Wars movies, which began in 1977. Yoda is a powerful and wise Jedi master who teaches many, including Luke Skywalker.

E.T.

In the 1982 movie *E.T.: The Extra-Terrestrial,* a friendly alien lands on Earth. A boy named Elliot becomes his friend and tries to help E.T. get home.

Superman

Stories of this DC Comics superhero became popular in the 1930s. He came to Earth when his planet, Krypton, was destroyed. He uses his strength and speed to save people in comic books, television shows, and movies.

Fact or Fiction?

Some real-life events make people worry that aliens are real. In 1938, Orson Welles did a pretend newscast on the radio. It was based on an 1897 book called *The War of the Worlds* by H.G. Wells. People believed the broadcast was real! Many became very scared and called the police.

Today, there are still news reports about mysterious crop circles and strange alien encounters. And, people continue to report **UFOs** shooting through the starry sky. So far, there is no proof that any of these are from aliens.

On the radio, Welles pretended aliens from Mars were taking over Earth.

In 1953, *The War of the Worlds* became a movie.

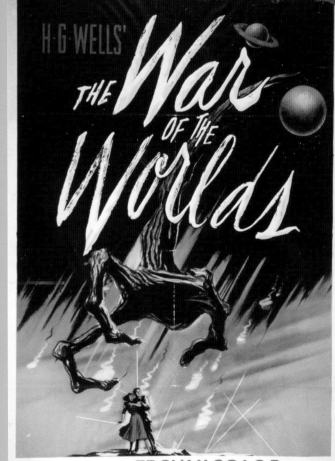

H·G·WELLS'
THE War
OF THE
Worlds

COLOR BY TECHNICOLOR

PRODUCED BY
GEORGE PAL · BYRON HASKIN · BARRE LYNDON · A PARAMOUNT PICTURE

DIRECTED BY

SCREEN PLAY BY

But, there are **rumors** about a place where there is **evidence** of aliens. It is called Area 51. Some people believe the US government studies and stores information on **UFOs** and aliens there. The government does say Area 51 is real. And, it does admit many secret activities happen there. But, it won't reveal exactly what.

Today, people continue to learn more about space. Scientists want to discover if aliens really do exist. There is no solid evidence, but there are lots of small clues and stories.

Rovers have been sending pictures from Mars since 2004. Some hope they will find evidence of alien beings.

Area 51 is in the desert near Rachel, Nevada. Some people believe parts of crashed UFOs, including the one from Roswell, are kept and studied there.

Extraterrestrial Highway
NEVADA 375

What Do You Think?

So, what do you think about aliens? Do they still send a chill up your spine? It can be fun to watch spooky alien movies or to dress as an alien on Halloween.

It is also interesting to learn about aliens. Knowing what is true and what is made up is powerful. Whether you read **fiction** about aliens or search for real-life **evidence**, you are in for an exciting journey.

Outer space may hold the answers to whether aliens exist.

Let's Talk

What examples of alien stories can you think of?

What would you do if aliens landed near your home?

How do you think it would feel to be an alien in a world not your own?

If you were to write a story about aliens, what would they look and sound like? Would they visit Earth, or would the story be set on a faraway planet?

Imagine that you were taken up in a spaceship. How would you talk to aliens?

Glossary

communicate (kuh-MYOO-nuh-kayt) to give and receive information, such as knowledge or news.

culture (KUHL-chuhr) the arts, beliefs, and ways of life of a group of people.

evidence facts that prove something is true.

fiction stories that are not real.

legend an old story that many believe, but cannot be proven true.

resource a supply of something useful or valued.

rumor a story that is passed from person to person but has not been proven to be true.

science fiction stories that deal with the future, space, time travel, and aliens.

species (SPEE-sheez) living things that are very much alike.

technology (tehk-NAH-luh-jee) the use of science for practical purposes.

UFO an unidentified flying object.

Websites

To learn more about Creepy Creatures, visit **booklinks.abdopublishing.com**. These links are routinely monitored and updated to provide the most current information available.

Index